Geckos

by Tammy Gagne

Content Consultant
Edward L. Stanley, PhD
Department of Vertebrate Zoology and Anthropology
California Academy of Sciences

Core Library

An Imprint of Abdo Publishing
www.abdopublishing.com

www.abdopublishing.com

Published by Abdo Publishing, a division of ABDO, PO Box 398166,
Minneapolis, Minnesota 55439. Copyright © 2015 by Abdo Consulting
Group, Inc. International copyrights reserved in all countries. No part of
this book may be reproduced in any form without written permission from
the publisher. Core Library™ is a trademark and logo of Abdo Publishing.

Printed in the United States of America, North Mankato, Minnesota
032014
092014

Cover Photo: Fedor Selivanov/Shutterstock Images
Interior Photos: Fedor Selivanov/Shutterstock Images, 1; Mikhail
Klyoshev/Shutterstock Images, 4; Shutterstock Images, 6, 9 (bottom),
28, 43; Biosphoto/SuperStock, 9 (top); David A. Northcott/Corbis, 10;
Animals Animals/SuperStock, 12, 14; Fabio Pupin/FLPA/Glow Images,
17; iStockphoto/Thinkstock, 19; Nancy Tripp Photography/Shutterstock
Images, 20; Thorsten Milse/Glow Images, 23; Cathy Keifer, 25; Glow
Images, 26; Red Line Editorial, 30; iStockphoto, 32, 34, 39, 45; Albert Lleal/
Minden Pictures/Corbis, 37

Editor: Mirella Miller
Series Designer: Becky Daum

Library of Congress Control Number: 2014932340

Cataloging-in-Publication Data
Gagne, Tammy.
 Geckos / Tammy Gagne.
   p. cm. -- (Amazing reptiles)
Includes bibliographical references and index.
ISBN 978-1-62403-372-8
1. Geckos--Juvenile literature.   I. Title.
597.95/2--dc23
                                            2014932340

CONTENTS

CHAPTER ONE
What Is a Gecko? 4

CHAPTER TWO
Growing Up Gecko 12

CHAPTER THREE
Gecko Nightlife 20

CHAPTER FOUR
Geckos around the Globe 28

CHAPTER FIVE
Geckos in Danger 34

Fast Facts 42

Stop and Think 44

Glossary 46

Learn More 47

Index 48

About the Author 48

What Is a Gecko?

It is an unusually warm summer night in the desert. A light colored gecko scurries through the sand. Its webbed feet help it move quickly and quietly. The gecko's wide eyes spot a cricket ahead. The gecko just woke up and is hungry. It needs to eat enough food and drink enough water before digging another hole in the sand to hide in during the day. The gecko catches the cricket and enjoys a nice snack. Suddenly

Geckos live in areas where they can blend into the surroundings, keeping them safe from predators.

Geckos absorb heat from features in their environment, such as sun-warmed rocks.

it hears a clicking noise. It's another gecko warning of a bird circling in the air. The gecko scurries behind a rock. The bird swoops down, and the gecko begins to croak loudly. The noise confuses the bird and it flies away. The gecko is safe!

Cold and Colorful

Geckos are reptiles. This group of animals includes other lizards, snakes, turtles, and crocodiles. Reptiles are cold-blooded. This means they do not generate enough body heat to keep themselves warm. They rely on external heat sources. Geckos and other reptiles often lie in the sun for this reason.

More than 1,500 species of geckos live in warm climates around the world. They can be found on every continent except Antarctica. Each gecko species is a little different. Geckos may have wide eyes, a large head, and a long or short tail. Many species are brightly colored, spotted, or striped. A gecko's coloring often matches its surroundings. This trait is called camouflage. Camouflage helps animals hide from their predators.

The web-footed gecko matches the reddish sands of Africa's Namib Desert almost perfectly. Tokay geckos live in India, China, and Southeast Asia. They have bluish-gray skin with red

Eyes Wide Open

Most gecko species do not have eyelids and cannot blink. A thin, transparent membrane covers the eye for protection from dirt and other harmful objects. Geckos lick their eyes to keep them clean. Even though their eyes are always open, they are still able to sleep.

spots. Giant day geckos live in northern Madagascar. They are bright green with red markings on their faces and bodies. Western banded geckos live in the southwestern United States. This species is cream, yellow, or pink colored. Their name comes from their brown stripes.

Sizing Them Up

Geckos vary in size. Most are fairly small. Scientists do not include geckos' tails when recording their length. They measure their bodies and heads only. Very few geckos are more than 5.5 inches (14 cm) long.

The New Caledonian giant gecko is the largest known living gecko in the world. It lives on an island off the eastern coast of Australia. These geckos are approximately ten inches (25 cm) long.

The Eyes Have It

Scientists now consider gecko species with eyelids a separate group from other geckos. These members are nicknamed eyelid geckos. They include the leopard gecko, the African fat-tailed gecko, and the Western banded gecko.

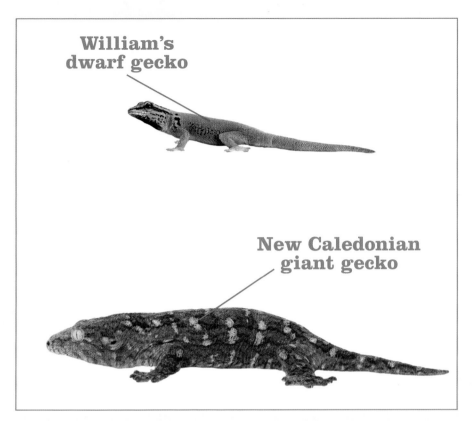

William's dwarf gecko

New Caledonian giant gecko

Blending In

This diagram shows two different gecko species. What type of environment do you think each gecko lives in? How do you think each gecko blends into its surroundings to hide from predators?

Several species compete for the title of smallest gecko. The gecko usually ranked as smallest is the pygmy gecko. Even as adults, these geckos only measure approximately 0.5 inches (1.3 cm) long. All gecko species range in weight from 0.8 ounces (23 g) to 1.5 pounds (0.7 kg).

The African fat-tailed gecko stores water and fat in its tail. This is useful since it lives in the desert.

Not Your Average Lizard

Like most reptiles, geckos have dry skin. Tiny scales cover their bodies. These scales protect geckos from injuries, such as cuts from sharp rocks. Scales also prevent heat loss.

Most geckos have special feet that make them great climbers. Their toe pads have thousands of tiny hairs called setae. These hairs stick to walls, ceilings, and wet rocks. But not all geckos get around this way. Approximately one third of all geckos do not have toe pads. They cannot climb as well as geckos that do have sticky feet. One gecko family lacks legs completely. They are called flap-footed lizards. They move by slithering like a snake.

A gecko tail can break off if it becomes stuck or if a predator grabs it. Over time another tail will grow in place of the old one. A gecko's tail helps it balance. Centralian knob-tailed geckos are named for the tiny, round lump at the ends of their tails. Scientists are not sure why they have this knob.

FURTHER EVIDENCE

There is quite a bit of information about geckos' bodies in Chapter One. What was one of the chapter's main points? What evidence was given to support that point? Check out the website at the link below. Choose a quote from the website that relates to this chapter. Does this quote support the author's main point? Does it make a new point? Write a few sentences explaining how the quote you found relates to this chapter.

Gecko Bodies
www.mycorelibrary.com/geckos

CHAPTER TWO

Growing Up Gecko

Like other reptiles, most geckos lay eggs. The majority of female geckos do not give birth to live babies. The amount of time it takes for the eggs to hatch depends on how warm it is. The warmer the air, the sooner the eggs will hatch. Most gecko eggs take between 80 and 120 days to hatch.

A female gecko lays only one or two eggs each spring or summer. The group of eggs laid by the

After a female gecko lays her eggs, she leaves the nest and does not return to raise her young.

Madagascar giant day geckos shed the outer layer of skin soon after hatching.

mother gecko is called a clutch. Once the female lays the eggs, her job is done. She does not sit on the eggs or protect the clutch. She does not care for the babies once they hatch. Male geckos do not care for their young either.

Baby geckos must take care of themselves from birth. They are born with strong instincts. These automatic behaviors help them survive. Baby geckos

can hunt for food as soon as they come out of
their eggs.

Baby geckos grow quickly. As they get bigger,
they outgrow their skin. New skin grows in from
underneath. A healthy gecko will shed its outer layer
of skin many times during the first months of its life.

Adult Geckos

Although some gecko species are highly social, most
do not live together. But they may interact with other
geckos when they see
them. Other species
prefer to spend most of
their time alone. Even
geckos that live alone
look for a mate once
they reach adulthood.
Reaching adulthood takes
different amounts of time
for each species. Climate
affects how fast a gecko

No Egg Needed

While most gecko species lay
eggs, not all do. Some species
give birth to live young
instead. New Zealand geckos
carry their eggs inside of their
bodies until they hatch. They
do not lay these eggs. This is
good for geckos that live in
cold environments. They can
carry their unborn babies with
them and keep them warm.

Female Species

Eight species of geckos are entirely female. One of them is the Bynoe's gecko from Australia. This species is able to reproduce without a male. Baby Bynoe's geckos are identical genetic clones, or copies, of their mothers. Other all-female gecko species include the Indo-Pacific gecko and the mourning gecko.

species matures. Smaller geckos in warm areas often mate before they are one year old. Larger geckos in cooler parts of the world may not reach adulthood until they are nine years old.

A male gecko in search of a female makes chirping noises. He does this to get the female's attention. He may also fight other males that court her. Geckos have teeth and will bite one another while pursuing a mate or to defend food or territory.

Most male and female geckos look similar. Males can easily identify females, however. They find them by their scent. In a few species, males and females are also different colors.

It can be hard to tell male and female pygmy leaf-toed geckos apart since they are the same colors.

EXPLORE ONLINE

The focus in Chapter Two is on young geckos. Gecko parents do not care for their young. The website below discusses how to care for a pet gecko. As you know, every source is different. How is the information given in the website different from the information given in this chapter? How is it the same? What new information can you learn from this website?

Gecko Care
www.mycorelibrary.com/geckos

Older Geckos

Geckos have a long life span. Leopard geckos usually live between 15 and 20 years. Some have even been known to reach 30 years old. Pet geckos often live much longer than wild geckos. Pet geckos do not have to worry about predators. Owners can also take pets to a veterinarian if they become sick.

Leopard geckos usually live between 15 and 20 years, but they may live even longer in captivity.

CHAPTER THREE

Gecko Nightlife

Most geckos are nocturnal. This means they are most active at night. They sleep during the day. Because they can close their eyes, it is easy to tell when geckos with eyelids are sleeping. But it can be harder to know when lidless geckos are snoozing. Geckos sleeping on the ground sometimes curl their tails around themselves for warmth. Gecko

Moths are just one of the insects geckos feed on.

species that live in trees can sleep and hold onto a branch at the same time.

What Does the Gecko Say?

Geckos are very vocal creatures. They communicate by making a variety of sounds. If a predator is near, a gecko may bark or chirp. They make this noise to frighten or confuse the other animal. Geckos also make clicking sounds to one another. Often they do this to warn other geckos about a predator. Males call to females using multiple clicks. Some females make noises in response.

Coming in for a Landing

Many people know about flying squirrels. But there are also flying geckos! Neither animal actually flies. But it looks like it sometimes. Flying geckos have flaps of skin along their head, neck, body, and tail. When they jump from a high place, these flaps help them glide slowly and safely to the ground.

The web-footed gecko has special feet to move quickly across sandy deserts.

Fast Enough

Compared to other lizards, geckos are not terribly fast. When running on flat ground, most geckos can only run at speeds of up to four miles per hour (6 km/h). When they climb, geckos move even more slowly. This is because of their sticky feet. The Namib day gecko is the fastest known gecko. This species has been recorded at a speed of

6.7 miles per hour (10.8 km/h). They can move 16 feet (5 m) in a single sprint.

On the Menu

A gecko's diet consists mainly of insects. Geckos are not picky. If they can catch it and fit it into their mouths, they will eat it. Spiders, beetles, and beetle larvae are among geckos' most common foods. Many geckos have even been known to eat scorpions. Some geckos also eat fruit and flower nectar when it is available.

The most surprising thing geckos eat is their own skin. When their old skin comes off, many geckos make a meal of it. Geckos have two reasons for this odd behavior. First, shedding skin takes a lot of energy. Eating the skin replaces some of the nutrients

Geckos eat almost any food that is available to them, including large insects.

A gecko will eat its skin so predators do not track the scent.

the gecko loses during the shedding process. A discarded skin can also be a clue for predators that the gecko is in the area. By eating the skin, the gecko protects itself from being discovered.

In a 2012 *Newsday* magazine article, journalist Kathy Wollard explains how geckos are able to walk upside down on nearly any surface:

> Each toe on a gecko's foot is covered with as many as 2 million microscopic hairs, each only as long as two human hairs are wide. At the end of each hair is an array of up to a thousand spatula-shaped tips, each about 200 nanometers (billionths of a meter) across. The tips are so small, researchers say, that the diameter of each is smaller than a wavelength of visible light.
>
> The advantage to all the microscopic structures: Gecko feet have millions of points of contact with a surface—from the rough bark of a tree to a smooth ceiling. According to recent studies, a million gecko foot hairs—which would fit on a dime—could lift 45 pounds. So it's easy-peasy for the hairy adhesive feet to hold a lizard running up a wall.

Source: Kathy Wollard. "How Come? Geckos' Insurance Is in Their Feet." Long Island Newsday. Newsday, July 9, 2012. Web. Accessed January 16, 2014.

Consider Your Audience

Read the passage above closely. How could you adapt Wollard's words for an adult or your classmates? Write a blog post giving this same information to the new audience. What is the best way to get your point across? How is your language different from the original text? Why?

CHAPTER FOUR

Geckos around the Globe

G eckos live on every continent except Antarctica. They live in warm climates throughout the world. Most live close to the equator, in the warmest parts of the world. But geckos can survive in many types of terrain. Their habitats include deserts, grasslands, jungles, mountains, and rain forests.

Tokay geckos can be found in the warm jungles of Cambodia.

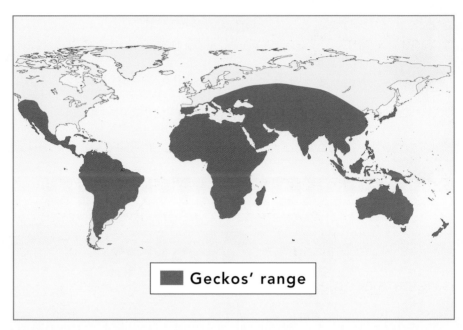

Gecko Ranges

Most geckos live in warm climates. This map shows where gecko species live throughout the world. Why do you think geckos prefer warm climates?

Australia has the most gecko species of any continent. More than 175 different gecko species live there. Madagascar has the next-highest number with more than 100 species. India ranks third with more than 90 species.

A Place to Call Home

Deserts are home to the highest number of geckos. Since some geckos are nocturnal. They can hunt when it is dark. Then they do not need to worry about staying cool or finding enough water. Rain forests and grasslands are two other common gecko habitats. Rain forests have many hiding spots. Grasslands have fewer areas where geckos can hide from predators or lay eggs. But they are full of good prey, such as insects and small animals. Even in rain forests, hunting is never a problem for geckos. They use their amazing climbing skills to track down food high in the trees.

How do geckos living in deserts survive without water? Geckos are able to get enough fluid from the insects they eat. Rare rain or even fog leaves moisture on many surfaces. Geckos lick the

First-Class Pets

Geckos are popular pets in the United States. They are also a common choice for classroom pets. Single crested geckos and leopard geckos are easy to care for. They are easy to feed. A ten-gallon (38 L) tank is large enough for one gecko. Even with the noises geckos make, neither species will disturb the class during study time.

The New Caledonian gecko uses its tongue to lick water droplets from its eyes.

water from those surfaces when this happens. Some geckos even drink the water that builds up on their own skin.

Geckos that live in the desert protect themselves from the hot sun by digging into the sand. The web-footed gecko uses its webbed feet to walk across the sand. Its webbed feet also help it dig into the desert dunes.

Natural Camouflage

If you are lucky enough to see a gecko in the wild, it may take you some time to notice it. Like many reptiles, geckos have natural camouflage. The Tokay gecko takes its camouflage a step further. It can lighten or darken the color of its skin. This helps it blend in with its environment even better.

My Shadow and Me

The Tokay gecko lives in trees and on large rocks in forests. It is brightly colored, but it can still hide from predators. It has a special way of blending into its background. These lizards have folds of skin that can stretch out over the bark of a tree. When the gecko does this, it does not cast a shadow. It simply blends into the bark of the tree.

CHAPTER FIVE

Geckos in Danger

Geckos' most dangerous natural predators are snakes. Other animals that hunt geckos include large spiders, birds, and various mammals. The biggest nonnatural threat to many gecko species is humans. As people use more and more land, many animals are left without homes. Even the New Caledonian giant gecko does not need large

If they do not hide in time, geckos in all habitats risk becoming a meal for a snake.

amounts of land. But it does need to eat and hide from predators.

When people drive animals from their homes, those species must move to new areas in search of food. If a type of snake is forced to move, it could lower the gecko population in its new location. If insect-eating animals are driven to a new area, they will be competing with the geckos there for food. If there isn't enough food to go around, some geckos could starve.

People take geckos from their habitats to sell so they can become pets. Other geckos are collected and killed to be used for medicine. In some countries,

While some geckos are nearing extinction, other species, such as the eyelash gecko, are being rediscovered.

people believe geckos are evil spirits. People kill them to get rid of these imaginary spirits.

Keeping the Species Alive

Several species of geckos are already extinct. A type of day gecko from the Mascarene Islands in the Indian Ocean has been extinct since the 1920s. A nocturnal gecko from the same area hasn't been seen since

1841. Scientists think a giant species from New Zealand is probably extinct too.

If more geckos become extinct, the insects that make up their diets could overpopulate certain areas. This could lead to a number of other problems. If these insects started feasting on farmers' crops, it could even affect the human food supply.

Hiding in Plain Sight

The leaf-tailed geckos of Madagascar are known for their highly effective camouflage. These eight species are nearly invisible in their natural habitats. As the name suggests, their wide tails look a lot like a tree's leaves. Their brown or green skin blends perfectly into the bark. Similar species live in Australia.

There are many gecko species on the critically endangered species list. Several more gecko species could become threatened if people do not make an effort to protect these animals' natural habitats. Defenders of Wildlife is a conservation group that

It is important for humans to take care of geckos and their habitats so more gecko species do not become extinct.

protects wild animals in the United States and beyond. This organization works with governments, businesses, and other groups to keep threatened and endangered species alive and well.

Gecko populations in the United States may not be at risk right now. But the best way to prevent that from happening in the future is to protect their habitats now. It is important for humans to continue preserving these amazing reptiles so they are around for many years to come.

In his book *Geckos: The Animal Answer Guide*, biology professor Aaron M. Bauer gives a small bit of hope for gecko species thought to be extinct:

> *While scientists' failure to find these geckos again may mean that they are extinct, it more likely reflects our lack of knowledge about the distribution and biology of the species. This can be seen in the case of the New Caledonian Crested Gecko. . . . This distinctive species was first described in 1866 and was reported to be common for about a decade after its discovery. Then it was not seen again for more than 100 years, despite many searches, and was considered likely to be extinct. In 1992, it was rediscovered and since then has been found to be locally abundant. It has since become one of the most widely bred and kept of gecko species.*

Source: "Geckos." Savanna Explorer. Savanna Explorer, n.d. Web. Accessed January 16, 2014.

What's the Big Idea?

Take a close look at Bauer's words. What is his main idea? What evidence is used to support his point? Search online for extinct gecko species. If you could rediscover one of them, which would you choose, and why? How does Bauer's work support the possibility of rediscovering a gecko species?

Common Name: Gecko

Scientific Name: *Gekkota*

Average Size: Less than 5.5 inches (14 cm), depending on species

Average Weight: 0.8 ounces (23 g) to 1.5 pounds (0.7 kg)

Color: Bluish gray, cream, yellow, pink, or cream

Average Life Span: 15 to 20 years

Diet: Mostly insects, spiders, and scorpions

Habitat: Deserts, grasslands, jungles, mountains, and rain forests

Predators: Humans, snakes, lizards, large spiders, birds, and various mammals

Did You Know?

- Most geckos can walk upside-down across ceilings.
- Most geckos do not have eyelids. Since they cannot blink, they lick their eyes to keep them moist.
- Baby geckos take care of themselves from the moment they hatch.
- Geckos live on every continent except Antarctica.

Another View

There are many different sources of information about geckos. As you know, every source is different. Ask a librarian or another adult to help you find a reliable source about geckos. Write a short essay comparing and contrasting the new source's point of view with the ideas in this book. How are the sources similar? How are the sources different? Why do you think they are similar or different?

Take a Stand

This book discusses humans destroying gecko habitats to create roads, houses, and businesses. Take a position on this practice. Then write a short essay explaining your opinion. Make sure you give reasons for your opinion. Give some evidence to support those reasons.

You Are There

Chapter Four discusses geckos' home ranges. Imagine you are vacationing in the Namib Desert. Write 300 words about your experience. What have you seen that helps geckos survive here? Is this habitat suitable for most gecko species?

Why Do I Care?

This book discusses why it is important to keep gecko species from becoming extinct. Even if you don't live near geckos, why should you care about protecting them? Write down two or three reasons humans should care about gecko populations.

GLOSSARY

camouflage
the disguising of something by changing the way it looks to make it match its environment

clutch
a nest or batch of eggs

equator
an imaginary line circling the earth that is equally distant from the north pole and the south pole

extinct
no longer existing

habitats
the places where a plant or animal naturally lives or grows

instincts
behaviors that are based on automatic actions

larvae
the young, wingless, often wormlike form that hatches from the egg of many insects

nocturnal
active at night

predators
animals that live by killing and eating other animals

transparent
fine or sheer enough to be seen through

LEARN MORE

Books

Bauer, Aaron M. *Geckos: The Animal Answer Guide.*
Baltimore: John Hopkins University Press, 2013.

Frazel, Ellen. *Madagascar*. Minneapolis: Bellwether
Media, 2013.

Hamilton, S. L. *Reptiles*. Minneapolis: ABDO, 2014.

Websites

To learn more about Amazing Reptiles, visit
booklinks.abdopublishing.com. These links are
routinely monitored and updated to provide the most
current information available.

Visit **www.mycorelibrary.com** for free additional tools
for teachers and students.

INDEX

camouflage, 7, 33, 38
Centralian knob-tailed
  geckos, 11
climbing, 10, 23, 31
cold-blooded, 6
communication, 6, 22
conservation, 38, 40
critically endangered,
  38, 40

diet, 24
dwarf geckos, 9

eggs, 13–15, 31
extinction, 37–38, 41
eyelid geckos, 8
eyes, 5, 7, 8, 21, 24

giant day geckos, 8, 24

habitat loss, 35–36
habitats, 7–8, 29–31, 36,
  38, 40
hunting, 15, 30–31

life span, 18

mating, 15–16

Namib Day geckos, 23
Namib Desert, 7
New Caledonian giant
  geckos, 8–9
nocturnal, 21, 30, 37

pet geckos, 18, 31, 36
pet trade, 36
predators, 6, 7, 11, 18,
  22, 26, 31, 33, 35, 36

range, 30

scales, 10
setae, 10
shedding, 15, 24, 26
size, 8–9
skin, 5, 7–8, 10, 15, 16,
  22, 24, 26, 32–33, 38

tail, 7, 8, 11, 21, 22, 36,
  38
threats, 35–38, 40–41
Tokay geckos, 7, 33

water, 5, 31–32
web-footed geckos, 7
western banded geckos,
  8

ABOUT THE AUTHOR

Tammy Gagne has written dozens of books about the health and behavior of animals for both adults and children. Her recent titles include *Great Predators: Crocodiles* and *Super Smart Animals: Dolphins*. She lives in northern New England with her husband, son, and a menagerie of pets.